ADDRESS

OF THE

HON. I. P. CHRISTIANCY

TO THE

GRADUATING CLASS

OF THE

Law Department

OF THE

MICHIGAN UNIVERSITY.

DELIVERED MARCH 28, 1860.

DETROIT:
BARNS, FRENCH & WAY, PRINTERS,
Nos. 52 and 54 Shelby Street.
1860.

Ann Arbor, April 4th, 1860

Hon. Isaac P. Christiancy :

Dear Sir—At a meeting of the Graduating Class of the Law Department of Michigan University, the following resolutions were adopted :

Resolved, That the address of the Hon. Isaac P. Christiancy, delivered at the late Commencement of the Law Department, before the first Graduating Class of the University, was well adapted to the occasion, and calculated, by its publication and dissemination, to work great benefit to the Law Department, in which all take a lively interest.

Resolved, That our committee be instructed to request Judge Christiancy to furnish this class with a copy of his address, for publication in pamphlet form.

Therefore, if you will have the great kindness to forward us a copy of your late address for that purpose, you will confer a great favor on the class of 1860.

Respectfully yours,

EDWARD P. PITKIN,
E. P. CLARK,
O. P. STEARNS,
Committee.

Gentlemen,—I have had the honor to receive, by the hand of Mr. H. Barns, your letter of the 4th inst., enclosing copy of resolutions adopted by the Graduating Class of the Law Department, and requesting for publication in pamphlet form, a copy of my address to the class at the late Commencement of that Department. Sensible as I am of its many deficiencies, yet the favor and kindness with which the class have been pleased to receive it, can not be better reciprocated by me than by complying with your request. I have therefore forwarded to you through Mr. Barns, a copy of the address requested.

With the highest esteem for yourselves personally, and the most earnest wishes for the professional success and individual welfare of every member of the class I am,

Very respectfully, yours,

I. P. CHRISTIANCY.

To Ed. P. Pitkin, E. P. Clark, and O. P. Stearns, Committee.

ADDRESS.

GENTLEMEN OF THE GRADUATING CLASS:

I congratulate you upon the advantages you have enjoyed here, the zeal with which you have availed yourselves of those advantages, the successful progress you have made, and the substantial evidence of that success you are now about to receive.

Each of you, as I am informed, had already spent some time in the same study, in the office of some practical lawyer, and some of you had already entered upon the practice of the law. You can, therefore, appreciate the difficulties and embarrassments attending the acquisition of systematic legal knowledge in that way, and the great advantages of an orderly and systematic course of instruction, such as you have just received here.

The law, like every other science, has its rudiments and its more advanced stages, its general principles and special departments, and hence a progressive system or order of development; and without due regard to some proper system of development, much of the time of the student is lost, and many of his strongest efforts rendered abortive.

While study in an office is essential to the

acquisition of ready, practical skill in the application of legal principles, and should therefore form a part of a practical legal education; yet the time and attention of the lawyer in active practice is generally, from necessity, occupied in so desultory a manner, to meet the exigencies of the various cases and business transactions thrown upon his hands, that he has little time to aid the student in any orderly course of instruction. The most he can generally do is to recommend a certain course of reading, and occasionally to inspect his progress. The student is therefore left mostly to himself in the pursuit of legal principles, and especially in their classification. And, though many do obtain a systematic knowledge of legal principles in this way, yet it is at the expense of much more time, and much greater effort; and, too often, the result is to make the student look upon the law as an art, rather than a science; to give a kind of a mechanical dexterity in the management of some of its machinery, than a broad scientific view of its principles. The dry rules of law, without reference to their reasons, are too apt to be mistaken for the law itself. The abstract rules of law, without reference to the reasons upon which they are founded, are merely arbitrary and technical. They are but the dry bones of the law, and represent the law about as faithfully as the dry, bony skeletons, to be found in another department of this institution, represent the living man.

There is a strong tendency in the human mind,

especially among those who do not like the labor of intense thought and close investigation, and who find it easier to resort to the stores of memory than to the reasoning powers, to mistake the mere scaffolding or the machinery of a science for the science itself; and the mode in which the study of the law is pursued in an office is not sufficiently calculated to check this tendency. The student is set to copying legal papers from drafts furnished him, or to drawing from, or merely filling up, printed forms, before he has sufficiently acquired and classified the legal principles which govern them. He is too apt to take it for granted that there is some mysterious potency in certain forms of words. He does not stop, and generally has not time, to analyze them, and to apply the principles of law which alone give them efficiency. The result is, that he often misapplies them; and when a pleading or other paper is to be drawn, for which he can find no form at all applicable, he is at once in the clouds. The same habit of mind leads him to stretch the application of abstract rules to cases not within their spirit, and which, upon principle, should constitute exceptions or qualifications; and when a question is presented for his opinion, to look for a precedent, rather than the principle which should govern its solution. If the case or the question, calling for his action, happen to fall strictly within some established legal formula, or to conform, in all respects, to some decided case, he feels strong. In preparing his case for trial, he hunts up his precedents and authorities with reference to a supposed state of facts; and if these facts come out as anticipated, it is all very well. But such is the perversity of human conduct, that most of it fails to proceed in straight lines, or in true curves, or at any regular or definite angles, and can not therefore be estimated by any geometrical lines or figures whatever. And cases are constantly thrusting themselves forward for decision, whose features exhibit a contemptuous disregard of all legal formulas, and which evidently never attempted to shape themselves upon the model of any decided case—cases in which the various ingredients of human conduct, rights and wrongs, and legal principles, are curiously mixed and blended together; the combined result of which presents a new compound, for which the chemistry of the law has yet established no fixed rule or formula, and which requires a new and independent analysis, to be framed from first principles. And these novel features and strange complications often present themselves, for the first time, upon the trial. The man of cases and precedents is then at fault, and gropes his way in darkness; for, though the principle which might illuminate his case, and guide him out of his difficulties, may glimmer feebly in the distance, his base of observation, his intellectual orbit, is too contracted to enable him to obtain a parallax, to determine its true position or his own, or to distinguish it from a thousand other twinkling luminaries which he sees scattered over the firmament.

Case lawyers are like pilots unskilled in the science of navigation, who succeed well enough while they hug the coast and keep the headlands in view, but are always in danger of being lost when they are driven beyond the sight of land. While he whose mind is well stored with the principles and reasons of the law—who, when a question is presented, instead of seeking first for a case, recurs at once to his own internal resources, determines what, upon principle, the law must be, and resorts to cases only for illustration and proof—such a man is ready for any emergency, and is never disconcerted when his case suddenly assumes a new phase. He finds, in the resources of his own mind, compass and quadrant, chart and chronometer, calculates his place, takes boldly to the open sea, and strikes directly for his destination.

Broad as is the field of legal science, he who aspires to eminence in his profession must not confine his attention to legal knowledge alone. The broader his field of observation, the more extensive his acquaintance with other branches of knowledge, the greater his prospects of success at the bar. Every science, every species of information, is more or less frequently brought into requisition. No other profession requires so extensive an acquaintance with the whole cyclopedia of human knowledge. It is therefore peculiarly appropriate that instruction in this science should be connected with the University, where the other sciences also are taught.

Nor is there any profession, the successful

practice of which, so imperatively requires a man's qualifications to come fully up to his pretensions; nor, in which it is so difficult, I may say impossible, to get a reputation for qualifications which he does not possess. The medical profession offers much greater facilities for quackery and imposture; but the truly scientific physician grapples with imposture under much greater disadvantages than the lawyer.

The professional duties of the physician are not generally performed in the presence, and much less under the scrutiny, of competent judges, and never under the eyes of those especially employed to expose his errors. And when, by chance or otherwise, the blunders of the incompetent, come to the knowledge of the scientific physician, he finds it perilous to expose them; for if the impostor have a fair exterior, a plausible address and a good share of tact, he will often, if not generally, succeed in persuading the majority to attribute to professional jealousy every attempt to expose his ignorance.

But there is no room for successful quackery in the practice of the law. Every effort of the lawyer, in the management of his cause, is subject to the closest scrutiny of competent judges. The eager eyes of opposite counsel are upon him, intent upon the discovery and exposure of his blunders. No base metal passes current here; groundless pretensions are unmasked; and, if the client has suffered by the errors of his counsel, the public are sure to know it. The quack phy-

sician may sometimes rely upon the discreet silence of the dead; but the quack lawyer can place no such reliance upon the discretion of the living.

It is quite a common opinion among the ignorant, that the practice of the legal profession is inconsistent with the obligations of conscience, or, that its tendency is unfavorable to strict integrity of character. I advert to this, not for the purpose of vindicating the profession from so groundless a charge, but to put you upon your guard against a class of men who sometimes disgrace the profession. There is a class of men who, without any love for, and mostly without any knowledge of the law, as a science, betake themselves to the law as gamblers do to cards, as a convenient means of filching a dishonest living; who either wantonly, or, which is nearly as reprehensible, by lending themselves to the worst passions of irritated litigants, stimulate and encourage litigation for the sake of a fee. They are generally men whose talents are admirably fitted for getting men into difficulties, but wholly unfitted for getting them out. Such men, happily rare among those admitted to the bar, are essentially knaves and pettifoggers, who, like the same class outside of the profession delight in neighborhood quarrels, and render litigation epidemic and malignant wherever they appear.

There are, also, occasionally to be found, I regret to say, men of rare talent and high attainments, but without moral principle, and recognizing no obligation which the law does not enforce, who resort to the law as hypocrites resort to the church, to perpetrate iniquity with less suspicion and greater success.

Both these classes, if they had not taken to the profession, as a cover for their villanies, would probably have taken to crime under a less respectable disguise.

The whole tendency of the study of the law, as a science, is to elevate and purify the mind, to give it acuteness and discrimination in the discovery of right and wrong, to inspire a love of Justice and equity, a hatred of wrong, injustice and oppression.

The science of the law is mainly the science of doing unto others, as we would that others should do unto us. Its chief aim is to enforce this principle of human conduct. True, it does not always perfectly attain this object. The aim of all men is happiness; but it is never fully attained in this world. The reason of the failure is the same in both cases. Man is an imperfect being, and all his laws, and all his efforts, will partake of his imperfections. There are shades and gradations of wrong which no human laws can undertake to redress; because these laws must be administered by men, and through the aid of human testimony. Nothing short of Omniscience can see the truth and the bearings of human transactions precisely as they are; nor judge, with certainty, all the motives of men. And he who acknowledges no higher obligation than human laws, proclaims himself a villain at heart, who, but for those laws, would not hesitate to commit the foulest crimes.

He who loves the law, as a science, keeping in view its ultimate object, will naturally, and almost necessarily, be an honest man. He will see, as all respectable members of the profession do see, that there is nothing, and can be nothing, in the duties of his profession, in any respect, inconsistent with the strict observance of truth and honesty, with the performance of every duty he owes to God, to society, or to any of his fellow men; that he is no more at liberty to violate any of these duties than other men; that there can be no such thing as inconsistent duties; that his duties to his clients are subordinate to the great cardinal duties he owes to God and to society; that his mission is to secure the triumph of justice, to detect, expose and crush iniquity; that knowingly to aid a client in the perpetration of a fraud, or the consummation of any wrong or injnstice, is to make himself equally guilty with the client, and a little more contemptible; since he becomes a mere hireling in wickedness. He will spurn every attempt to secure his aid in the prosecution of a claim, or the maintenance of a defence, which he knows to be fraudulent or unjust; and if, in the course of a cause, he discovers that he has been unwittingly entrapped into such a position, he will refuse to proceed, and leave the client the responsibility of selecting less scrupulous counsel.

Counsel are, no doubt, often deceived by the

false statements of clients, and induced to believe the client an honest and injured man, when he is but a designing knave. Such clients will seldom be induced to reveal their nefarious schemes to respectable counsel, as they can not hope to enlist his sympathies in their behalf.

But the strong sympany which counsel will naturally feel for those who seek his aid and his zeal to protect them from injustice, doubtless have a tendency to make him slow to believe anything to his client's prejudice, and to look upon all testimony against him as false or suspicious, when it does not appear in the same light to others. In this way, his zeal for the right may sometimes make him an unconscious instrument of wrong.

Compelled, as counsel generally are, to get their first ideas of a case from the statements of their respective clients, opposing counsel, in the great majority of cases, do sincerely believe ther respective clients in the right, and the opposite party in the wrong. Each of the opposing parties, also, not unfrequently thinks himself in the right; while it is evident one must be mistaken, and perhaps both; for many law-suits originate in honest mistake: and self-interest blinds the eyes of parties, as zeal and sympathy do the eyes of counsel. And if it be true, that zeal for a client, and a natural pride of success, will sometimes lead even respectable counsel, in the heat of conflict, to pass the line of perfect rectitude, and, for the moment, to think more of the success than of the justice of his cause—a fault more common with the young than with more experienced counsel—this is only to say, that lawyers are not exempt from the ordinary frailties of men; and like other men, no doubt, they repent of such errors when the heat of the conflict is passed, and reflection has taken the place of excitement.

The first duty of the professional lawyer is that of a peace-maker, to calm the excited passions, to check the vindictive feelings of clients, and to bring them back to reflection. Every experienced member of the profession knows that the amount of litigation would be doubled, often the peace of families, sometimes of neighborhoods and whole communities, disturbed, and a state of intestine warfare kept up, by a general neglect of this duty—by counsel simply lending themselves to the dishonest schemes and exasperated passions of clients. No urging would be needed; simply following is enough to produce this result.

No honorable lawyer will ever advise litigation where substantial justice can be obtained without it. He will never try a cause till every reasonable effort for settlement has been exhausted; nor will he ever advise a client to insist upon the utmost strictness of his legal rights; he will rather advise him to forego some portion even of his equitable rights for the sake of peace.

If we were at liberty to consider this question without any reference to duty or to morals, as a simple question of personal policy, it would still be found that this course of practice will, in the end, be most advantageous to the practitioner.

It will inspire confidence, and secure the best class of business. He might not make money so rapidly at the outset. Doubtless money may be more rapidly obtained, for a time, by larceny or highway robbery, than by honest means; but this mode of making money is not likely to succeed long, nor to become permanently profitable. Few crimes are more injurious to society than that of encouraging wanton litigation. And he who can no where find professional employment, without encouraging litigation, may safely conclude that he has mistaken his vocation, that society does not need his professional aid, and that he had better turn his attention to some other means of support.

But no man is at liberty to regulate his professional conduct by considerations of profit and loss only.

Every individual, all classes of men, in all the relations of life, have duties to perform, duties to each other and to the society in which they live; and the duties of every individual, and of every class, are in exact proportion to the power and influence of the individual or the class. Every augmentation of power or influence brings with it additional and corresponding duties. And, as the legal profession possess more power over the whole field of litigation than any other class, so are they under a corresponding obligation to exert that power for the good of society. And the same may be said of the influence which, as a class, they possess in moulding and improving the laws and institutions of the country in which they live.

I shall not undertake to enumerate all the various duties and obligations of the profession; they are well understood, and, I am glad to believe, generally observed by the reputable members of the profession. But, as all these duties and obligations grow out of the position occupied by the profession with reference to the society at large, it may not be amiss to consider what that position is.

The only just, philosophical view which can be taken of this subject is this: that the profession constitutes one of the great departments of human labor for the common good.

Every branch of knowledge, as well as every variety of physical labor, is brought into requisition for the supply of human wants, and the promotion of the social welfare. But, as in physical labor, no one individual can ever acquire sufficient dexterity in every variety of occupation, and a division of labor enables each to attain greater practical skill in his particular department, and thus increases the aggregate product; so in the field of mental labor, it is impossible for any individual to acquire that complete familiarity with every branch of knowledge, and that practical skill in its application, which are necessary to any high degree of success; and hence the necessity of a division of mental labor.

Thus, for illustration: the human body is a complicated and delicately constructed piece of mechanism, liable to numberless derangements known as diseases, almost infinitely varying in type and intensity, and often approaching and blending with each other. To cure these diseases, the peculiar characteristics of each disease, and, to some extent, of each individual constitution, must be studied; and the effects of the various kinds of medicines, and other curative agencies, must be ascertained. Here is the study of a lifetime, a demand for the knowledge which has only been acquired through the accumalated observation and experience of successive generations, and the safe, practical application of which necessarily becomes a specialty. This is the province of the physician.

To correct, by persuasion, by appeals to the judgment and better feelings of men, the natural tendency of the passions to excess, to soften their asperities, to purify and elevate the affections, to teach us to love justice and mercy for their own sake, to make us better in all the relations of life, and to alleviate the afflictions incident to our condition, with the hope of a better life hereafter—these objects require special qualifications and discipline. Here is the province of the clergyman.

But such is the tendency of the human passions and propensities to run to excess, and in default, as well as in defiance of moral and religious teaching, to resort to wrong and violence; and so liable are men, even with the best intentions, to misapprehend each other, and to understand, in a different light, the same transaction, that every community, as it emerges from barbarism, where force alone decides, must have fixed laws for the protection of right, and the redress of wrong.

And, as in civilized society, business transactions, social relations and duties, become almost infinitely various and complicated, and the more so, the more civilization advances—so, in corresponding ratio, must the laws which apply to and regulate them, become various and complicated also. To ascertain the nature of these various transactions and duties, their relations to each other, the principles involved in, and the laws applicable to each—to acquire that thorough knowledge and accurate discrimination necessary to a ready, practical application of those laws, in such a manner as to secure the rights of parties and the public welfare—to accomplish this requires years of careful study and preparation. This is the province of the lawyer.

All these professions or departments of mental labor, and many others, are necessary to the full development of civilized life, and, when properly directed, all work harmoniously together for the common good.

It is this tendency which must always determine their legitimacy, and measure their utility.

All these professions, like all other departments of labor, and all the faculties of the mind, are liable to abuse. Should the physician, to gratify his own or another's malice, or to acquire or give to others the means of perpetrating some other crime, poison or drug his patient instead of curing him—should the lawyer make use of his professional talents to promote schemes of robbery and fraud, on his own or another's account, or stir up litigations for the sake of business or a fee—should the clergyman become a wolf in sheep's clothing, and for selfish or mercenary ends, countenance vice, because it is popular, sanction and encourage injustice or oppression, because it is strong, and spurn its victim because he is weak, take advantage of the confidence his position inspires, to sap the morals of his flock, and lure the unsuspecting into crime, or inculcate hatred and bitterness, instead of kindness, mercy, peace and good will to men—then, in these several cases, the physician, the lawyer, the clergyman, equally perverts the end and object of his profession, and, instead of performing its duties, abuses its privileges.

The present might be deemed a proper occasion to indulge in some words of practical advice to those who are preparing to enter upon the practice of the profession for the first time. But the forty minutes which I had prescribed to myself are so nearly expired, that I shall not be able to say much upon this head. And if I had the time, yet knowing the qualifications, the experience and fidelity of your Professors, I should enter this field with the greatest diffidence. But there are two considerations, generally considered of minor consequence, but which I deem of so much practical importance, that at the risk of repeating what may already have been said, and better said, by your Professors, I will take the liberty of suggesting them.

Most of you, who have not yet entered upon the practice, will probably, before doing so, spend some time in the office of some practicing lawyer. While so employed, and afterward, when you engage in the practice for yourselves, let me caution you against falling into the habit of trusting too much to printed forms or precedents, or, to any forms prepared by others. It will be much better to accustom yourselves to the drawing of pleadings and every kind of legal instrument, entirely from your knowledge of legal principles. After having completed the paper in this way, if not entirely certain of its sufficiency, then, for the first time, consult some approved form. This will furnish suggestions, and serve to test your accuracy. Let this process be repeated until fully satisfied of entire correctness. This course will seem slow and laborious at first, but it will become easier at every attempt; and it is the only course which can ever give ready practical skill in this department of the profession. It compels and keeps up familiarity with legal principles and the modes of their application, induces the habit of looking to the substance, rather than the forms of things, and makes a scientific lawyer rather than a legal mechanic.

Many young men of good talent have settled down into third-rate lawyers, because they found it so much easier, at first, to avail themselves of forms ready drawn, than to go through the necessary labor and thought of preparing them. In yielding to this seductive habit, they have saved labor, but dwarfed the intellect. They have relied upon crutches till they are unable to walk alone.

It is hardly necessary to say, that when you have once acquired a ready facility in drafting legal papers, you may safely resort to printed forms as occasion may require.

Another very common error with the young man, just commencing the practice of the law, is his anxiety to do too much business at the outset. His motto, at this stage of his professional life, should be, to make haste slowly. He is just beginning to apply his store of legal principles to actual practice, to real transactions, as they arise. He has already acquired, perhaps, the dextrous use of the foils, and the highest skill in feigned combats; but he is now to enter the earnest conflict, to wield and to ward the naked steel. The utmost circumspection is necessary, and his progress at first must be slow and cautious. He should see clearly the bearings of every question in the case or transaction he undertakes, and of all the legal principles involved, arranging and classifying everything in its proper place.

Every succeeding case, every item of business done in this thorough and methodical way, will increase his facility, and he will find himself progressing with accelerated speed. But if he take upon himself, at once, more than he can thus thoroughly and systematically perform, his store of legal principles may become confused and disarranged before he has acquired a reasonable facility in their use; his mind may become bewildered, and he may find himself forgetting rather than improving. To use terms borrowed from the printing office, his stock of legal principles may be thrown into pi before they are well locked in the form.

One suit thoroughly and ably managed is worth more to the young practitioner than ten carelessly conducted; not only for the reasons already stated, but because much of his reputation and prospects may depend upon his early efforts. It may take some time to overcome the effects of a false step in this stage of his career. The public sometimes decide too hastily, and do not always make sufficient allowance in such cases.

But I must hasten to a conclusion.

That there is, to-day, a graduating class in the law department, shows that a second important epoch in the history of the University has, at length, been inaugurated. The medical department had already proved a complete success, and its beneficial effects have, for years, been felt by that profession and the public.

As the laws upon which man's physical health and physical existence, as an individual, depend, seem naturally to take precedence of those which regulate his rights and duties in relation to others and to society, it was, perhaps, fitting that the establishment of the medical, should precede that of the legal department.

But the law department has now, also, become a fact accomplished; and, contrary to the common experience of such institutions, it has had no infancy, no childhood. It sprung at once into complete efficiency and vigorous manhood. This, to some, has been a matter of surprise: but for myself, I thought it had become a public want: I knew your Professors, and I anticipated the result.

To all who feel an interest in the advancement of science and the dissemination of knowledge in our State, as well as to the Regents, and the Professors in this institution, and to you, gentlemen, it must be a matter of congratulation, to see the University of Michigan rapidly becoming what its name imports, and what the public interest requires, an institution which shall afford, within itself, full and complete instruction in every branch of human knowledge. But to none can this be more gratifying than to the able, zealous and efficient officer who presides over this institution, who has for years so patiently and perseveringly, through good and through evil report, and in the face of all discouragements, labored with so much success to bring about this result. When assailed he did not reply: when reviled he reviled not again; but his works have spoken for him.

www.ingramcontent.com/pod-product-compliance
Lightning Source LLC
LaVergne TN
LVHW011143110826
845150LV00008B/2478